30 NEW DAYS ALCOHOL-FREE

FOR SOBER CURIOUS DRINKERS

Fay Kortleven

Forward

30 New Days Alcohol-Free – For Sober Curious Drinkers is your guide to finding out where alcohol fits into your life. It is for those sober curious drinkers who wonder if they are drinking too much.

30 New Days Alcohol-Free was created for the mother who longs for wine o'clock, but worries about her health. It was written for the newly divorced woman who wonders if sinking into a bottle of wine at night is really helping her cope or not. It is for the women who wonder if they are being held back by their need for a drink when things get tough. It is for the women who want to know where alcohol fits into their lives. And, it is for those who secretly worry that they are drinking too much, and worry about if they can cope without a drink or three.

30 New Days Alcohol-Free was created with kindness for all women who are interested in exploring what life without a daily wine or a weekly binge looks like.

Introduction

Are you curious about what your life looks like without drinking? For me, this question came from a deep desire to know what it was like to be fully present in the hard moments and not numbed by the buzz of a glass of wine.

My curiosity about being alcohol-free lasted for much longer than 30 days. After almost a year without drinking, I thought I had satisfied my questions. So, I decided to reintroduce an occasional glass of wine back into my life. I thought I had found the place where alcohol could fit into my life in a breezy, easy way that I could take or leave.

After a couple of months, my drinking began to retake parts of my evening. I felt the anxiety that I was drinking too much again. I would lie awake at night, worrying about where alcohol fitted into my life. So, I recommitted to another 30 days without alcohol to explore this further. This time I took notes, journaled and recorded the experience while writing 30 New Days Alcohol-Free to guide others on the same questioning journey.

30 New Days Alcohol-Free is the latest of my 30 New Days books that began with the Moving on Strong Journal – 30 New Days of Renewal and Reinvention After Divorce. My 30 New Days books encourage women going through difficult times to view each day as a fresh new opportunity to move towards their goals. The focus on 30 NEW days reminds us to leave behind the stumbles of yesterday and instead focus all our energy forward. You can find out more about the other 30 New Days books at www.30newdays.com.

In 30 New Days Alcohol-Free, each day begins fresh with new optimism, excitement, and strength towards our goal of 30 days.

This book will not make you feel bad, beat you up, or pile on the guilt if you slip up over the next 30 days. If you want to stop halfway, take a break from the detox and then restart, you can.

I have written 30 New Days Alcohol-Free with compassion, kindness, and complete understanding that making a change is not always a smooth process. We start, we stop, we change our minds, and so the cycle goes. 30 New Days Alcohol-Free is here to support you in this exploration of being alcohol-free for a month. It is here to remind you each day that you are stronger than you think, wiser than you believe and more amazing than you can fathom.

Each day, you will be encouraged, given new ideas and support for coping with any alcohol cravings. Included are daily writing prompts to encourage you, deepen your experience and help you find out more about yourself and your relationship with alcohol. This book is written to help you explore your relationship with alcohol, and includes ample space to write, reflect, and record your journey.

At the end of each week there is space to reflect on the week before, how you are feeling, how you are sleeping and any other physical or emotional changes you have noticed. This reflection page is a great way to look back and see what the benefits of this journey have been for you. Be excited by this; share it with others who are also wondering about the place of alcohol in their lives.

Over these 30 New Days I will:

Remember that each day is a new start

Always focus forwards

Put intention into action each day

Be open to the possibilities of each day

Be kind to myself

Let myself off the hook if I misstep or miss a day

YOU ARE
STRONGER
THAN YOU
THINK,
WISER THAN
YOU BELIEVE
AND MORE
AMAZING
THAN YOU
CAN FATHOM.

QUESTIONS ABOUT BEING SOBER CURIOUS

Questions About Being Sober Curious

What Is Sober Curious?

If you think you might have a problem, but you are not sure if it requires giving up alcohol altogether, you likely fall into the sober curious category. You might be in the habit of comparing your drinking to those around you. Perhaps you wonder if you are an alcoholic or not, based on the level of your friends' drinking. Everyone has their own relationship with alcohol, and taking a break from alcohol for 30 days can give you a chance to look at your relationship with drinking and where it fits into your life. 30 New Days Alcohol-Free gives you the space and time to ask yourself the important questions about drinking in your life:

Is drinking keeping you from being your most productive self?
Is it standing in the way of your goals?
Is it interfering with your relationships?
Are you generally unhappy?
Think seriously about that one: are you unhappy?

This period of exploring life without regular drinking gives you the chance to examine where alcohol fits into your life.

What If I Fail?

Guess what? If you slip up and have a drink over the next 30 days, that's fine. The whole point behind 30 New Days is forward momentum towards the goal. We do not get hung up on a mistake or misstep from the day before. We just start each day as new again and continue with our plan. The aim of this journey is to experience being alcohol-free for 30 days. By committing to this goal each day, you will be able to re-examine where drinking fits into your life.

Try not to put too much pressure on yourself. There does not need to be a black and white line between success and failure. You only need to decide that you are going to follow this journey for 30 days. Make that decision and take it one step at a time from there. If you make a mistake or have a drink in this time, you can learn what triggered you, and keep growing and developing on your path to understanding where alcohol fits into your life or if it doesn't. Don't let the fear of failure keep you from trying.

Can I Still Go Out?

Removing the habit of drinking can mean changes to your social life for a few weeks. There may be times when events that used to be fun now feel long, dull and boring without a drink in your hand. There's no way around that. But rather than drink your way through dull events, consider the option of not going to these events and places for this short time. It might mean that you prefer to be a little less social while you explore this journey. It may require some new strategies for the next 30 days.

Going alcohol-free for 30 days lets you decide how you want to spend time and with whom you want to spend it with, freeing you from the loop of drinking to get through situations you don't want to be in. Use this time to explore other alcohol-free events that you may have rejected in the past.

But If I don't Go Out, What Will I do?

In theory, all this extra free time will help you stay focused and achieve your dreams. You may find you not only have a lot more free time on your hands, but you also have a lot more energy. Use this double bonus of time and energy to do something new, learn a new language, get ahead at work, go to the gym, read, draw or paint.

Be kind to yourself and enjoy activities that excite you, bring you joy or get you closer to your goals.

How Will I Relax?

For many of us, wine o'clock was the time of day when we could finally relax. Trying to relax without a glass of wine in the evening is going to feel like a challenge, but consider that you will have more space for quiet clear-headed thinking time. If this isn't your thing, here are some distractions to help you relax without a wine:

Find a new Netflix series to follow

Sign up for a physically active class

Follow an intense yoga class on YouTube

Meditate with a guided meditation and mindfulness session

Throughout this journal, you will find lots more ideas and advice on how to relax and enjoy these 30 days without alcohol.

Will I Lose All My Friends?

When you stop drinking for a period of time, other drinkers may be disappointed to lose their drinking buddy. If your friends are big drinkers, they may be disappointed that you aren't boozing any more, and for the next 30 days, those probably aren't the kind of people you should hang out with. Surround yourself with people who respect your decision. Your choice to try 30 days without alcohol is not something you should have to justify to anyone. It is your choice to do this, and only you need to know why you want to explore the place alcohol has in your life. Your friends who love you will support you.

Will I Miss Out On All The Fun?

We all have that FOMO (fear of missing out) that comes at certain times. It could be at a wedding or event where everyone else is drinking, or it could simply be a Friday night when you would usually open a bottle of wine at home with your partner. For the next 30 days, you will have times when you feel like you are missing out, and a glass of wine may be hard to resist.

Think about what you are actually missing out on. You are skipping the temptation to drink too much, you are skipping waking up with your head pounding, with spotty memories and a vague feeling that the whole night went sideways.

These next 30 days are your chance to give yourself a full break from alcohol and find other ways to treat yourself.

These 30 days are about learning how to relax and find enjoyment without a glass of wine or three.

Throughout the next 30 days, this journal will show you how to really be kind to yourself and it will encourage you on this journey.
Be ecstatic that you have found the time and courage really to examine the role alcohol plays in your life. You get to check for sure if your drinking is a problem or not over the next 30 days.

Will I Be Boring?

If alcohol has become too important in your daily life, these 30 days will be a great way to adjust that. If you have relied on alcohol to make you feel funny, happy, give you courage or let you relax, you will be able to find new ways to tap into those feelings without a drink.

You are brave enough to stop drinking for 30 days, and through this 30-day journal, you will explore how to be more present and excited about life with or without drinking.

Will I Have To Explain My Sobriety All The Time?

Just having to explain that you are wanting to take a break from alcohol can be exhausting. If you want to share the details of your sobriety, it's great. If not, here are a few simple things you can say if questioned about your personal choices:

No thank you, I'm not drinking.

I used to drink, but I don't right now.

I drank for a long time, and it was really fun. Then, it wasn't fun anymore, so I stopped.

I'm just taking a break at the moment.

I'm driving.

YOU CANNOT
CHANGE
YOUR
DESTINATION
OVERNIGHT,

BUT YOU CAN
CHANGE
YOUR
DIRECTION
OVERNIGHT.

GETTING STARTED

Getting Started

As you head into this 30 New Days alcohol-free journey, you might be feeling some anxious anticipation. You may be worried about how this will work. It is likely that you are already concerned about an upcoming event that involves drinking. You may be tempted to put this journal down until after that event. These are all normal feelings before starting a detox of any kind.

Put your worries aside for now and just get started on the journey. This journal is written to support you through the next 30 days and help you figure out how to navigate any difficulties you might come up against. If you haven't already, read the previous section that addresses some of these concerns.

Over the next 30 days, expect to be very surprised at the changes that will come. Some of the best things you will find are being much more clearheaded in the morning. You will begin to feel better, lighter and have much more energy. There may be a noticeable reduction in your anxiety levels as your natural happiness increases. You can expect to notice that you are more open to new things, and your relationships may improve as well as your emotions.

Starting Point Reflections

Before beginning this 30 new days alcohol-free journey, take some time to record how you feel. Circle the number that best reflects where you are on the scale right now.

Unhappy	1	2	3	4	5	**Happy**
Bored	1	2	3	4	5	**Excited**
Trouble Sleeping	1	2	3	4	5	**Sleeping Well**
Stressed	1	2	3	4	5	**Calm**
Unhealthy	1	2	3	4	5	**Healthy**
Unproductive	1	2	3	4	5	**Productive**

How do you feel about starting 30 New Days Alcohol-Free? Write down your feelings here:

What are you worried about? Write down any thoughts:

What are you excited about? Write down your thoughts:

Week One

DAY ONE
LET'S
BEGIN

Day One: Let's Begin

Welcome to the first day of your Alcohol-Free Journal. Today, at the beginning of this journey, you might be feeling a mixture of excitement and worry. You have likely come to this point after deciding that there is something about your drinking that bothers you. You might be interested to see how you feel after 30 days without alcohol. This may be the beginning of a journey into complete sobriety, or it might be a simple exploration of how it feels not to drink for a month. Either way, welcome to the first day. Together, we are going to journey through the next 30 days alcohol-free and see where the journey takes us.

Today, we lay the groundwork for the rest of your journey.

Write down your reasons for beginning this 30-day alcohol-free journey:

What prompted you to begin?

Why now?

Have you tried to stop drinking before?

What happened?

What are you looking forward to finding out during these 30-days alcohol-free?

Faith is taking
the first step
even when you
cannot see the
whole staircase

- MARTIN LUTHER KING

DAY TWO

BUILDING EXCITEMENT

Day Two: Building Excitement

I hope you are feeling the excitement of trying something new – bubbling enthusiasm that you are making a positive change in your life. Today is a new day! I hope you are looking forward to it.

One of the best ways to set yourself up for success in a 30-day detox is to build a personal toolkit. This toolkit is a collection of things that will help you get through the times when you crave a drink. You can include items in your toolkit that will help you to resist any cravings.

It is important to have a toolkit of things that will keep you focused and relaxed and that will actually help you to enjoy this journey. Of course, I have lots of ideas and suggestions for you! You can find an extensive list at the back of this book.

SOME OF THE ITEMS I USED IN MY TOOLKIT:

Music
A great playlist on my phone that I can play to boost my mood when I am walking, driving or just feeling a little bored.

Chai latte
I have a large packet of chai latte powder in my cupboard. I find it super yummy to sip in the evening. I have also found a fab green tea latte that is currently my all-time favorite drink to sip any time of the day.

Your list might include your favorite tea, hot chocolate mix or any other warm drink that helps you to relax in the evening without a glass of wine. Go ahead, treat yourself to something different over these next 30 days.

Tonic water or sparkling water
I use a sodastream machine to make bottles of sparkling water to sip in the evening or with my dinner.

Bubble bath, bath oils, bath bombs

However you like your bath, load up on the goodies to make it. For me, relaxing in a bubble bath was a huge help to get over a craving for a glass of wine in the evening. A bath is also fantastic for getting your mind and body ready for a good night's sleep.

Yoga and meditation

Yoga is another fantastic way to relax and be present in the moment. It encourages you to feel your body and focus on your breathing.

Meditation can help in the same way. During my first 30 alcohol-free days, I was not in the mood to go out to a group class. So, I found a great YouTube channel and lay my yoga mat out in my living room in the morning sun to practice. Try it out!

Great books

I have included a list of fantastic books that can help and support you with making changes in your life. My two favorites are: *This Naked Mind* and *Quit Like a Woman.*

Blogs

I have also included at the back of this book a list of challenging and interesting blogs that I like to read. They offer lots of fab tips and ideas for the sober curious.

Netflix

Binge-watching Netflix over the next 30 days is completely allowed. Make yourself a large glass of lime and sparkling water and put your feet up.

Walking/running

Getting your body moving over these 30 days will help boost your happiness vibe. I love to walk first thing in the morning while listening to a podcast or my favorite playlist.

At the back of this book is a sample Detox Survival Toolkit with a list of lots of great ideas for your personal toolkit. Have a look through and choose some of the best ones to add to your own.

My Detox Survival Toolkit will include:
List 10 items that you can add to your personal toolkit.

1.

2.

3.

4.

5.

6.

7.

8.

9.

10.

Did you use any tool from your Detox Survival Toolkit today? What was it, and how did it work out?

WHAT YOU GET
BY ACHIEVING
YOUR GOALS IS
NOT AS
IMPORTANT AS
WHAT YOU
BECOME BY
ACHIEVING
YOUR GOALS.

ZIG ZIGLAR

DAY THREE

BEYOND WILLPOWER

Day Three: Beyond Willpower

As we head into day three, you might be feeling the strongest pull of cravings. On this day, the feeling of missing out on something can be strongest, and you may be using all your willpower to resist just grabbing a drink. Day three can feel hard!

When we hit a day like this, our minds start to remind us of all the good times we had when drinking. We remember all the reasons why we want to drink. This is normal throughout these 30 days, especially during the first week.

The key to change is to reframe the story in your mind. We can use willpower only for a limited amount of time to resist cravings and give something up for a few days. To get beyond the power of our wills, we need to change the loop in our brains.

It is time to reframe the story you tell yourself about why you are taking a 30-day break from drinking. It is important to focus our attention on the good that we hope to gain from this experience.

We start by focusing on the negative effects that we are avoiding. This is a list of things that we did not like about drinking.

Here is my list:

I like that I wake up feeling better.

I love that I don't feel groggy in the morning.

I don't miss the feeling of tiredness after a few glasses of wine.

I like that I can remember everything about my evening.

I love knowing that I have not said or sent messages that I don't remember.

Write your list:

Add anything you recall from drinking that may have led you to pick up this book and commit to 30 days without alcohol. You might be missing out on post-drinking binge-eating, blackouts, arguments, drunk crying, unsafe driving, lack of focus at work, or feeling depressed. Whatever added to the decision to stop drinking for 30 days, write them down.

Now that we are avoiding all of these things for the next 27 days, we have a lot more time and energy. What are you going to do with all that extra time and energy? Some people use this month as the kick-start towards a project they have always wanted to do; write that book or start training for that half marathon. This 30-day break from alcohol is a fantastic time to improve your health, mood and energy levels.

Turn your attention away from missing alcohol and towards setting some new goals or plans.

Write down a few ideas for new goals or plans that immediately come to mind. If you feel enthusiastic about this, make a more detailed list. If you are not feeling the enthusiasm yet, do not worry. Tiredness and a low mood on day three are also entirely normal. Mark this page and come back to it when you feel more upbeat about this 30-day journey.

Positive things I could be doing instead of drinking over the next 27 days:

Your comfort
zone keeps
expanding every
time you get out
of it

REFLECTION SPACE

SCRIBBLE, DRAW OR WRITE WHAT'S ON
YOUR MIND TODAY

DAY FOUR

CREATING A SOBER CURIOUS MINDSET

Day Four - Creating A Sober Curious Mindset

A sober-curious mindset is very helpful to achieve a 30-day alcohol-free goal. A sober curious mindset means coming into this journey with a sense of adventure and excitement. It allows you to lean toward the process and be open to what you will discover about yourself.

If you are focusing only on the negative part of removing alcohol, you will experience these 30 days like a trial or punishment, making your journey a lot harder than it needs to be.

With a sober-curious mindset, we flip the script in our minds. We start to focus on what we are gaining, rather than what we are giving up. By journaling each day, you can discover more about your strengths and where alcohol fits into your life going forward.

This journey can be life-changing, if you let it.
The sober curious journey is about questioning many of your core beliefs around drinking. It helps you to look at why you drink, when you drink, and what triggers you to drink. By stepping back from drinking for 30 days, you can gain a better perspective on your drinking habits and past experiences with alcohol. The key is to be open to the process of learning more about yourself as you go through each day.

The following sentences are written from a sober-curious perspective. Highlight any that you agree with and then write some of your own:

I am curious to see how I will feel after 30 days without alcohol.

I am curious to learn what triggers me to want a drink.

I am curious to know how my energy levels will be after 30 days.

I am curious to know if I will notice a difference in my appearance after 30 days.

I am curious to know if I will notice a difference in my attitude to alcohol.

Write your own sober curious sentences:

I am curious to know:

I am curious to know:

I am curious to know:

I am curious to know:

Reminder: Have you completed the starting-point reflection worksheet at the beginning of this book? Reflection pages are an excellent tool for tracking your energy and mood over this 30-day journey.

THE JOURNEY
OF A
THOUSAND
MILES BEGINS
WITH ONE
STEP

- LAO TZU

DAY FIVE

HOW TO BE SOCIAL WITHOUT DRINKING

Day Five: How To Be Social Without Drinking

Many 30-day challenges encourage you to post about it publicly on social media using a hashtag etc.

Personally, I don't think you need to do anything publicly unless you want to. Going alcohol-free can be a liberating and exciting journey that you want to share with everyone. It can also be a very personal time of self-questioning your past relationship with alcohol.

This journey is yours. You get to choose when, where and how you share this with others. But also feel comfortable about holding this journey as private, sacred and something you do alone.

One of the hurdles we can face over these 30 days is an anxiety about socializing without alcohol. This can be especially strong if we are someone who has built a social life around being out with friends drinking.

If you are feeling a little unsure about attending an event where you will be drinking, it is OK to back out of it. You are absolutely allowed to avoid going out for the first few days or weeks of this journey. This is your journey! The key is ensuring you set the pace. I wrote this book specifically for those of us who do not like to be pushed or bullied into something we are not ready for. This journey is about going at your own speed.

If you are eager to get out with friends without the temptation of drinking, use this time to find ways to have new, fun experiences with your friends that do not revolve around alcohol like a movie, an art class, a yoga class, a walk on the beach, a swim, the gym, a book reading, or a play.

Hang in there: you will get into the swing of going out without drinking in your own time. It can be a very enlightening experience to be out without drinking.

Take note of how it went, how you felt, and what you noticed. Write about the experience in your journal as part of your sober-curious research. And, enjoy waking up the next morning feeling fantastic, instead of hungover.

What worries do you have about going out and not drinking?

What thoughts go through your mind about not drinking in public?

How can you overcome these worries?

What steps could you take to avoid going out if you don't feel like it?

Or what steps could you take to go out and not drink?

Will you tell others or keep it to yourself?

TIPS FOR HEADING OUT TO AN EVENT

Before you go out, first consider an easy exit strategy from the event. My first few times going out without drinking were not difficult, but they were incredibly dull! The evening can feel very long and tiring when you do not have a wine buzz. The easy way out is to tell others that you have to be up early in the morning, you are tired from a busy week or that you have to relieve the babysitter early. Any excuse that allows you to cut out early if you want to will do.

When you get to the event, see if you can spot others who are not drinking. They are probably the ones sipping a long time on a full glass of wine, or drinking sparkling water. It is good to know you are not alone! More and more people are choosing to skip alcohol and still enjoy a night out with friends at the bar.

Get yourself a cool, refreshing drink to sip. There are lots of options available on menus that actually taste very nice.

Great Alcohol-Free Alternatives

Sparkling water - with mint, lime or straight

Alcohol-free beer or wine

Mocktails

Lime soda

Fresh juice

Fresh mint tea

Cassis

Cranberry juice

NOTES FROM THE FIELD

First Social Outing Without Drinking:

Date:

Event:

Description:

How did it feel not to drink?

Who was there?

Did they comment on you not drinking?

How was that?

What did you observe as others drank? Anything of note?

How did you feel?

How did it go?

Other notes from the event:

Personal suggestions for next time:

I CANNOT GIVE
YOU THE FORMULA
FOR SUCCESS,

BUT I CAN GIVE YOU
THE FORMULA FOR
FAILURE

WHICH IS:

TRY TO PLEASE
EVERYBODY

REFLECTION SPACE

SCRIBBLE, DRAW OR WRITE WHAT'S ON
YOUR MIND TODAY

DAY
SIX

SUGAR
CRAVINGS

Day Six - Sugar Cravings

One of the most significant changes you might have noticed over the last five days is how much sugar and carbs you crave. Some people feel a massive surge in sugar cravings in the first two weeks after they have stopped drinking. These cravings can be especially intense in the evening, resulting in a nightly chocolate or chips binge.

The good news is that these intense cravings for sugar usually dissipate after the first two weeks as it is simply a matter of your body adjusting to the change. Knowing that this is a temporary thing can help you ride through it without getting too hung up on the extra calories you might be indulging in.

During this sugar-craving stage, I enjoyed letting myself off the hook about snacking. I was already doing a great thing for my body by detoxing from alcohol that I considered it OK to indulge a little extra on my favorite chocolate or crisps for a few days. Consider it a soft reset and let yourself munch on crisps or sweets if this helps with the wine cravings.

Be kind to yourself. You are doing super well.

Have you noticed that your eating habits have changed this week?

How do you feel about this?

How does it feel to let yourself indulge more on sweet things?

Are you enjoying or hating the process?

Write a little about how it makes you feel.

You are doing a great job and are almost at the end of the first week.

Use the space below and on the next page to write about how it feels to be on day six:

REFLECTION SPACE

SCRIBBLE, DRAW OR WRITE WHAT'S ON
YOUR MIND TODAY

Sometimes we don't realize our own strength until we come face to face with our greatest weakness

-SUSAN GALE

DAY SEVEN

HELLO GRUMPY

Day Seven – Hello Grumpy

These early days of detox can bring out the morning grumps. Some of us feel an intense irritation towards the people we live and interact with daily. On these days, even the littlest things can drive us crazy. If someone is making too much noise in the morning or talking too much, we can lose the plot. Sometimes it can feel like your skin is just prickly, if anyone gets too close.

This is entirely normal in these first few days. There is an irritation that comes with any change or detox. You are changing the patterns in your life, and there will be days when everything rubs you the wrong way. As we are at the end of the first week, today is a great time to focus on how to handle these irritations.

Clear your space
Find ways during the day to clear more space around you. Try to take a few minutes to clear the clutter from your desk, your benchtop or around your home. Wherever you are working each day, try to make it as clutter-free as possible.

Alone time
Carve out time in your day to be alone and without interaction. Finding quiet time is easier said than done when you have small children or a busy job, but it is essential for your recovery. Getting up a little earlier to fit in a morning walk can give you some time alone before you start the day. Even taking a longer shower can be enough to give you a little extra space. Instead of rushing your shower, stand for a little longer, feel the water running over you and focus on being completely present in the moment. And just breathe.

How can you clear some space in your day today? Write down some ideas.

How can you create some alone time in your day today? Write down some ideas below.

Get busy

Irritations can be caused by pent-up energy that has no place to go except towards getting irritated with the next person who walks through your door. Instead of channeling your irritation towards others, get busy on a task that you can complete and feel a sense of satisfaction from finishing. This could mean getting outside in the garden and clearing away those leaves, or tidying that back porch. Or, you could pick a room in your home that needs a revamp and get busy decluttering it. Finding small tasks that can be completed in an hour or two is a fantastic way to keep busy and moving forward during this detox time. And, like the sugar cravings, this feeling of irritation will pass over the coming days.

What tasks can you complete in one hour that would feel great to get completed?

What task can you do today?

LIFE IS:

10%

WHAT HAPPENS TO
US

AND

90%

HOW WE RESPOND
TO IT

WEEK
ONE
REFLECTION

Week One Reflection

Unhappy	1	2	3	4	5	Happy
Bored	1	2	3	4	5	Excited
Trouble Sleeping	1	2	3	4	5	Sleeping Well
Stressed	1	2	3	4	5	Calm
Unhealthy	1	2	3	4	5	Healthy
Unproductive	1	2	3	4	5	Productive

Describe this week in a few words:

What did you struggle with?

How did you overcome these struggles?

What were the happiest moments of this week?

What did you achieve?

What have you learned about yourself this week?

What would you like to improve next week?

Anything else:

For the next week, I am excited about:

Next week I am looking forward to:

Next week I will be kind to myself and treat myself in the following ways:

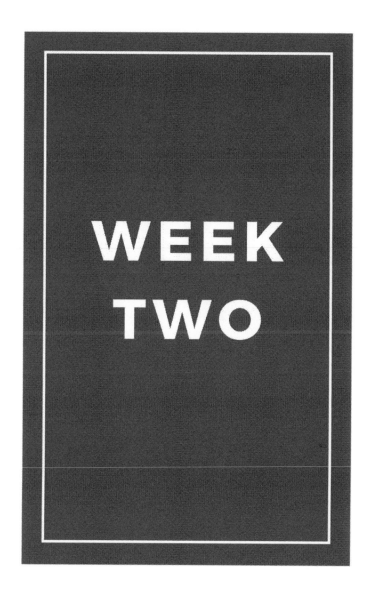

Week Two

THE SECRET OF GETTING AHEAD IS GETTING STARTED

WEEK TWO: WHAT TO EXPECT

Week Two: What To Expect

Week two can be an interesting time in your detox. Your body has been completely cleared of alcohol, and the more intense physical cravings have passed. Your mind, however, is a different matter.

Part of you will be feeling great about having achieved one week without a drink; another part of your brain might be strongly suggesting that you can now have a wine to celebrate. This dual thinking is called dissonance. It is when you are holding two contradictory ideas in your mind at the same time. In this case, you hold the idea that you want to complete 30 days alcohol-free, but you also want a drink. Therefore, either drinking or not-drinking is an action that goes against one of these ideas.

Annie Grace in her fantastic book *The Naked Mind* explains that while you may consciously desire to abstain from drinking, the intense craving in your mind can remain strong and make it hard to think of anything else. Your mind continues to hold the idea that having a drink will provide enjoyment or ease your stress. Therefore, when you are on a detox for a few weeks, you will experience this intense feeling or desire for a drink, which goes against the commitment you have made to yourself to try 30 days without a drink.

How do we cope with this?

As with most things, recognizing the pattern is vital. Notice when you experience a craving. Allow yourself to feel the sensation of it and acknowledge it as part of this journey. Then, let it pass through you, without taking any action on it. Giving in to a craving can leave you feeling deflated and disappointed with yourself. As we head into week two, we turn up the extreme self-care practices, we accept that cravings are going to happen and we keep going. You are doing awesome!

Did you feel any cravings for a drink today?

How did you cope with the craving?

Were you able to let the craving pass through you without acting on it?

What actions could you take next time you feel a craving?

Each
new day
brings
with it

new

possibilities

DAY EIGHT

RESISTANCE STOPS CHANGE

Day Eight - Resistance Stops Change

Our natural resistance to change has the power to stop us from making the changes that we want. As humans, we are wired to resist change. Taking a break from alcohol can be a dramatic adjustment to our usual patterns. The best way to overcome resistance is by taking each day, step by step. Like a writer choosing to sit and write each day, waking up and committing to another day without drinking is a daily choice that can feel hard in the beginning, but becomes more natural when it becomes part of our regular pattern. Every day you put between you and the last drink makes the next day easier to resist any cravings.

The buzz of getting through the first week can lead to some intense cravings. Many of us feel like having a drink to celebrate! It is important to remember that the first week of detox is the hardest, as you are pushing against physical and mental resistance. Now the physical cravings will have dissipated; what is left is the cravings in your mind.

You have completed one week without drinking! So, feel the power of that achievement and celebrate by being more determined to get through today too. You are on a good run now! Do not waste the effort by giving up on day eight. Do not be tempted to repeat those first three or four days of physical cravings by reintroducing alcohol to your system now. Continue forward and onward to find out the benefits of 30 full days without alcohol.

When do you feel the greatest resistance to this 30-day journey?

What do you do when you feel this resistance to change?

Can you reframe this resistance as a positive thing?

How can you resist the cravings today?

What strategies will you put in place?

What strategies worked for you last week?

How can you celebrate the end of one week without alcohol? (Without alcohol!)

Positive things from today:

DAY NINE

THE COST OF CHANGE

Day Nine - The Cost Of Change

Making a change for the better always has a cost. Recently, I watched a program about a man who lived in a house on a dangerous corner where cars would speed past precariously close to his window. Over the years, a large number of cars actually crashed through his kitchen window. Because of these accidents, he now lived in constant fear of his life, and avoided going into the kitchen as much as possible. Against all logic, he remained living in this house simply because he felt that the cost of moving was too high. He would rather stay in this house, in a constant state of fear, than move and lose money.

Watching this poor man and his calculations about the value of his happiness and peace against the financial loss of selling his house cheaply and moving made me realize that we all do this to a degree. Some of us cannot change the patterns we live with because we have calculated the cost to be too high.

Is there a cost to stopping drinking? Yes. You might consider it a cost that you cannot have a glass of wine in the evening, or join your friends for a round of drinks at the bar. But what is the cost of letting alcohol control your decisions?

What have been the costs of change during this alcohol-free period?

Is there anything you think you are missing out on?

What do you hope to gain?

**What positive outcomes are you hoping for over these 30 days?
List a few:**

Are the costs of change during this 30-day detox worth pushing past to get to the end? Why/why not?

Are your calculations accurate?

Are you putting too much value on the costs and not enough on the gain?

How much is the feeling of achievement worth to you?

How important is it to regain your life balance?

What worth do you place on the peace of mind from not drinking?

Is it worthwhile to ensure that alcohol is no longer the centerpiece of your life?

What are these things worth to you?

What is the cost of worrying about your drinking?

Do you lose sleep worrying about your drinking?

What is the cost of spending the night lying awake wishing you hadn't drunk so much, or wondering if you are drinking too much too often?

What is the cost of feeling emotional, out of control, hungover, angry, and/or tired?

Has your drinking cost you extra time and energy that could have been used for other things? If yes, give an example.

Has your drinking cost you extra money? How much over a period of time?

Has your drinking cost you any part of your health? I.e., did your drinking make health problems more difficult or add new ones?

Has your drinking cost you parts of your relationships? If so, with whom and how?

Add these costs to the equation when you are thinking about the cost of change and what you perceive as the cost of stopping drinking.

Write down your conclusion: Is it worth the perceived cost to continue with this 30-day journey?

These can be painful things to think and write about. Take extra time today to be kind to yourself. Run a large bubble bath or take yourself for a walk in the evening to relax before bed.

GOOD THINGS HAPPEN ON THE OTHER SIDE OF HARD

DAY

TEN

LETTING GO

Day Ten - Letting Go

Letting go of drinking, even for 30 days, is not a peaceful release for everyone. For many, it can be an intense confrontation of who they were and who they want to be.

You are allowed to feel scared or uncertain at times. It is entirely normal to feel split in two minds: one wanting to keep drinking and the other wanting to experience this journey to the end.

Letting go of the image of who we are when we drink is hard. If drinking made you feel social, powerful, outgoing, it is confronting that image to imagine yourself without drinking.

This 30-day journey is a chance to try a different life. It is about unpacking your reasons for drinking, taking a step out of that pattern so that you can look back on it with clarity and know if it is something you want to return to or not.

To stop drinking for 30 days is also a journey inward. It requires looking at your motives. Take some time to write down your thoughts to the following.

What makes you want to drink?
Who, what, when, why, and/or where?

Why do you like to drink?

What is your story about you and drinking?

Is it a story that needs to change?

Are you writing a new story? What is it?

Change is OK. Find the good in it. Move forward into the coming days with strength. You have this. Be bold, be brave, be sure.

YOU CANNOT
REACH FOR
ANYTHING
NEW WHEN
YOUR HANDS
ARE FULL OF
YESTERDAY'S
STUFF

DAY
ELEVEN

STICK WITH IT

Day Eleven - Stick With It

Setting the goal of 30 days without drinking is the easy part. Sticking with it is where it gets complicated.

Perhaps you have tried to stop drinking in the past, but had given up?

This time is different. You can get through these 30 days because there is no beating yourself up if you slip up or make a mistake.

There is no perfectionism on this journey. It is merely 30 new days alcohol-free. If you miss a day, there is no need to throw in the towel. Instead, wake up the next day and face it as a completely new day. You do not need to bring the mistakes from the day before into the new day. Each day starts fresh and new.

Each day is a step towards success. A step in the wrong direction is not a disaster. It is not a landslide that means you have to give up and start over. It is a chance to reflect and see if there is something you need to change to help you make a better choice next time.

Over these 30 New Days I will:

Remember that each day is a new start

Always focus forwards

Put intention into action each day

Be open to the possibilities of each day

Be kind to myself

Let myself off the hook if I misstep or miss a day

Today is a great day to take a look over your coping methods for change. It can be that in the middle of focusing on this detox journey, life will throw you a curveball: you get sick, your job gets extra busy, or you have a family emergency. Having great methods to cope with stress and change is crucial to getting through a detox period.

Take a look at the Detox Toolkit section for some great ideas on how to cope with unexpected hurdles along the way. By getting in the habit of reaching for healthier options when we feel like a drink, we can build ourselves up, find courage in our choices and not sink into the numbness of a glass of wine to deal with difficult times.

If you have been choosing to drink whenever you felt terrible, sad, or let down, this part of the journey is an enlightening time to discover different ways to support yourself, connect with your emotions and cope without a drink. It creates a way to remove the need for alcohol as a crutch, a numbing agent or a mood-booster.

Pick three new ideas from the Detox Survival Toolkit section at the back of this book. Write them here:

How might you try to use these ideas in the coming days?

What strategies can you use to distract yourself from cravings?

What strategies on the list might help you to de-stress in a healthier way?

What strategies can you use when you find yourself overthinking things?

What strategies can you use when you want to opt out for a while?

Know the strategies that are available to you. Get them ready and use them. Finding new ways to deal with stress, cravings, and general curveballs life throws at you is a fantastic learning experience that can help you many times more.

What steps are you taking today towards success?

KNOWING OTHERS
IS INTELLIGENCE;

KNOWING YOURSELF
IS TRUE WISDOM.

MASTERING OTHERS
IS STRENGTH;

MASTERING
YOURSELF IS TRUE
POWER.

- LAO TZU

REFLECTION SPACE

SCRIBBLE, DRAW OR WRITE WHAT'S ON
YOUR MIND TODAY

DAY TWELVE

EMOTIONS

Day Twelve – Emotions

Detoxing can feel raw. Our emotions are closer to the surface when we are changing life patterns or habits. In the past, you had a glass of wine or a stiff drink to calm your nerves, relax or to switch off. Without the numbing effect of alcohol, our emotions can feel much stronger, especially in the first few weeks. This change is a great thing and not something we should be worried about. You are now experiencing your full range of emotions without hindrance or being numbed by alcohol. When you experience a strong emotion, try this technique:

Describe how the emotion feels:

Where do you feel it in your body?

Look at that part of your body and see for yourself that there is no physical harm happening. The emotion is not doing anything to harm you. Nothing has changed physically.

Let the emotion slip away; it is doing you no harm.

As the emotion fades, recall how it felt to feel it. Write your description of the emotion:

How did it feel when it first hit?

Where did it spread in your body?

What thoughts came to mind?

This technique of analyzing our emotions can help us to understand that they are simply feelings. We can choose how we react and what we do about them. Practice this technique each time you feel an unwanted emotion coming over you.

Emotions cannot do you any harm.

They are harmless feelings.

You are still whole.

You are still safe.

Feelings have no potency.

They cannot physically hurt you.

In the same way, we can start to tune into the positive emotions we feel.

Try this technique of being fully aware of positive emotions:

When you are hugging your partner, child or a friend, focus entirely on the emotion you are feeling.

Let it fill you, flow over and around you.

Hold the feeling.

Try to control this feeling and bring it back to mind just by thinking of this moment again.

" In order to move on, you must understand why you felt what you did and why you no longer need to feel it."

-MITCH ALBOM, THE FIVE PEOPLE YOU
MEET IN HEAVEN

DAY THIRTEEN

NATURAL HIGHS

Day Thirteen - Natural Highs

When we don't drink, our bodies are able to regulate our hormones and endorphin levels better. Our bodies are experts at regulating these levels, but too much alcohol in our systems can cause all sorts of problems with this.

Now that you are near the end of week two without alcohol, your body is starting to adjust your levels at a healthy pace again. Over the first few days after your last drink, you would have been more aware of your emotions. As described yesterday, you may have a low feeling hanging around you at this time. You might find that you feel a little down and are spending too much time dwelling on things from your past that you are not happy about. This lower mood is a normal process of removing alcohol from the driver seat of your emotional levels. Understand that your body is working hard to bring everything back into balance. This emotional rollercoaster will end soon enough. But, in the meantime, make sure to find time to be awesome to yourself. Do things that you love to do. Take as many bubble baths, naps, ice cream bowls, or hours of binge-watching Netflix as you want.

One way to combat this low mood is to take some time to focus on the positive possibilities all around you. There are thousands of things that could go amazingly well for you in the next 24 hours. It is a great exercise to make a list of all the things that could go surprisingly well for you in the next day. These things can be as outrageous and unlikely as you want. Though, it can be fun to see how many things on your list do actually happen.

Make a list of 20 things that could go amazingly well in the next 24 hours for you.

This list can include things like: I get a raise, I find a lost item, I meet up with an old friend, I make a new friend, etc.

Come back to this list often to circle the ones that actually happen.

"THE ONLY
PLACE
WHERE YOUR
DREAMS
BECOME
IMPOSSIBLE
IS IN YOUR
OWN
THINKING."

— ROBERT H SHULLER

DAY FOURTEEN

RETHINKING OUR DRINKING

Day Fourteen – Rethinking Our Drinking

There are so many beliefs and ideas we hold about drinking. During a detox period, these thoughts can become loud, conflicting and confusing. Sometimes we need just to clear them all out. Journaling is a great way to get these thoughts out and on paper. Other great ways to process your thoughts are with art, talking with a friend or exercising.

A large part of this journey is about looking back on our drinking and seeing things in a new light. Perhaps you look back and cringe at the way you used to drink, or maybe you have memories of unwise decisions you made when you were drinking? These thoughts will come up and there will be many strong emotions connected to these. But, there is no benefit to beating ourselves up over past mistakes around alcohol. Your past is what led you to this journey.

Letting go of your history with alcohol and stepping into the next two weeks with positive energy is essential.

Write down eight things that you want to let go of from your past. This list could include pent-up anger, frustration, guilt; or anything that causes negative energy. Write them down here:

1.

2.

3.

4.

5.

6.

7.

8.

Now that you have these eight things listed, choose a way to imagine them gone:

Imagine casting these thoughts or ideas into the sea.

Let them drift out of sight on the ocean.

Imagine throwing them up into the air and watching the wind scatter them far away from you.

Write down these eight items on small pieces of paper.

Tear up the paper and put it into a bowl.

Take the bowl outside into your garden and set the papers alight.

Watch them burn and watch the smoke drift into the air.

Set yourself free by watching the paper burn to ashes.

Then, scatter the ashes or mix it with some water and pour it away.

Make a conscious decision not to get so caught up by the negative energy of these things again.

Draw a line under each item on the list that you are done with. Release yourself from any guilt around these things. Stop any thoughts of, 'I could have done it differently'. You made choices at the time that made sense to you then. Don't fill your mind with rethinking all of this.

Forgive yourself

Release any guilt

Let go of the past

Let's move on.

THOUGH NO ONE
CAN GO BACK AND
MAKE A BRAND
NEW START,

ANYONE CAN
START FROM NOW
AND MAKE A
BRAND NEW
ENDING

- CARL BRAND

WEEK TWO REFLECTION

Week Two Reflection

Unhappy	1	2	3	4	5	Happy
Bored	1	2	3	4	5	Excited
Trouble Sleeping	1	2	3	4	5	Sleeping Well
Stressed	1	2	3	4	5	Calm
Unhealthy	1	2	3	4	5	Healthy
Unproductive	1	2	3	4	5	Productive

Describe this week in a few words:

What did you struggle with this week?

How did you overcome these struggles?

What were the happiest moments of this week?

What did you achieve this week?

What have you learned about yourself this week?

What would you like to improve next week?

Anything else:

For the next week, I am excited about:

Next week I am looking forward to:

Next week I will be kind to myself and treat myself in the following ways:

Week Three

WEEK THREE: WHAT TO EXPECT

Week Three: What To Expect

You are now halfway through the 30 New Days Alcohol-free journey. Some of the stronger physical cravings for alcohol will have stopped, your energy levels will be slowly returning to pre-drinking levels, your sugar cravings may be less intense, and your mood may be much lighter. For some, these feelings are not so obvious yet. Don't worry; they will come.

As you enter week three, feel proud that you are at the halfway point and still moving forward. Great job! Let's jump into this week with positivity as we start to feel lighter, happier and more positive about this journey.

DAY FIFTEEN

OVERTHINKING YOUR DRINKING

Day Fifteen - Overthinking Your Drinking

One of the main reasons many people remain sober beyond 30 days is the relief they feel. They no longer have to think about their drinking anymore. While this can be hard to comprehend after only two weeks, ultimately deciding not to drink again removes the need to think about moderating, counting your drinks or wondering if you have had too many. You never have to hide how much you are drinking, or try to stretch a drink when your friends are not drinking as fast as you.

Were you at times worried about how much you were drinking? Describe these times:

Were you at times worried about the regularity of your drinking? Describe these times:

Have you at times been worried about your behavior when drinking? Describe this:

In **what other ways did thoughts about your drinking take up your mind space?**

Did it take a lot of mind space thinking about trying to last for a few days without a drink, or to resist the urge to have a drink earlier than usual on a Friday?

Consider how much time and mind space thinking about your drinking takes.
Now that you are halfway through 30 alcohol-free days are you thinking more or less about alcohol?

How does it feel? Has there been a shift in any way?

As you go through the next 15 days, keep these questions in mind. Notice if you begin to feel a little relief at not having to think about drinking all the time.

You have made your decision to make it through these 30 days, and with that decision, you do not need to make a daily or hourly decision about drinking. You have decided to make this journey; now, the key is not to question your decision.

Sometimes it is the smallest decision that can change your life forever

-KERI RUSSELL

DAY SIXTEEN

WAVES OF EMOTIONS

Day Sixteen - Waves of Emotions

Angst, anger, frustration, sadness – we are human, and we feel all of these feelings. Drinking does not help you to deal with any of these emotions. The only way through an emotion is to go through it.

Learning and growing past depending on alcohol to deal with negative emotions is a positive change. We are creating new pathways in our brains to deal with stress, anger, sadness and any 'negative' emotion that can trigger our, 'I-need-a-drink' urge.

Think of how you used drinking in the past to numb some of the more painful times of your life. Perhaps it was after a funeral, or during a breakup or a major upheaval in your life? Consider the times you reached for a drink to cope with your feelings.

Did drinking get rid of your painful feelings and thoughts at the time?

Did it help you to get rid of your painful feelings and thoughts over the long-term?

Did drinking help you to move past a painful experience positively?

Was your drinking helping you to create a positive and fulfilling life?

If your answer to some of these questions is no, we can then consider that drinking offered no benefit in a difficult time.

"IT IS ONLY IN
OUR DARKEST
HOURS THAT WE
MAY DISCOVER
THE TRUE
STRENGTH OF THE
BRILLIANT LIGHT
WITHIN
OURSELVES THAT
CAN NEVER, EVER,
BE DIMMED."

- DOE ZANTAMATA

DAY SEVENTEEN

A NEW WAY FORWARD

Day Seventeen – A New Way Forward

Pushing pause on our drinking can bring up a lot of memories of times we were not so proud of our behavior when drinking. In this journey, it is essential not to beat ourselves up about something that happened in the past. This journey is about moving forward and finding new and positive ways to get on with our lives. It is about finding the place where drinking fits, or doesn't fit, into our lives.

Think back to one of the more vivid memories of a time you let your drinking control a situation.
Reimagine that time, without the drinking.

How would you have behaved differently?

How would you have talked differently?

What else would have been different?

How would you have treated others differently?

How would you have treated yourself differently?

Which version of you do you prefer?

Today, take time to be extra kind to yourself. This journey can bring up a lot of emotions and thoughts. It is worth the time to look after yourself with kindness through this journey.

I think one day you'll find that you're the hero you've been looking for

-JIMMY STEWART

DAY EIGHTEEN

FEELING INCOMPLETE

Day Eighteen – Feeling Incomplete

We have grown to believe that drinking relaxes us, makes us feel great, gives us confidence, gives us a buzz, and so on. It is, therefore, normal to think that we will not be able relax without a drink or that we need a drink to be having fun.

Overcoming the belief that we are not complete without a drink is one of the hardest parts about a 30-day detox. It can feel like we are missing out.

Instead of focusing on these things, today, we will focus on the positive things that come from giving your body a break from drinking. Many of the benefits of being alcohol-free will start to show up now. You may start to notice some of the little changes that happen around this time.

Have a look in the mirror.
Do you notice any changes to your face? Some people see the whites of their eyes are whiter. Others notice there is less puffiness in their face, in particular around their eyes. Perhaps your skin is brighter and has a more beautiful color to it?

Take note of some of the changes you notice:

Have you noticed you are less bloated?

Are you feeling more positive or focused during the day?

How has your mood changed?

How are you feeling about getting to day 18?

Is this the longest you have gone without drinking? How does that feel?

There is so much to gain from taking this break from alcohol. It is great to take time to notice the difference in your body. Stop throughout the day to notice the little changes that come without drinking.

Keep a note of them here:

Focus on the journey, not the destination.

Joy is found not in finishing an activity but in doing it.

-GREG ANDERSON

DAY NINETEEN

ULTIMATE SELF-CARE

Day Nineteen - Ultimate Self-Care

Some days we need to make our only focus taking care of ourselves in the best way we can.

These are the days we need to go back to bed and get that extra hour of sleep we desperately need. These are the days we need to create a small nest on the sofa with a warm drink and a good book or a Netflix series, and just let ourselves stop for a few hours. These are the days we need to let others pick up the slack. These are the days we do not worry about being perfect or having everything under control. These are the best kind of days for some of us.

Be super kind to yourself these next few days. Detoxing can feel overwhelming, and the desire to reach for a glass of wine to take the edge off will be at its highest now. Distract yourself with kindness by doing the little things you would not usually take the time to do.

As women, we often put our own needs lower in the priority list. During this detox, raise your needs. Make it a number one priority. That means if you want to take a bubble bath in the morning instead of a shower, do it. If you want to have a little nap in the middle of the day, do it. If you want to curl up on the sofa with a good book and a box of chocolates, do it. Permit yourself to do anything that is going to make you feel a little better, except reaching for a drink. Extreme self-kindness is fantastic and an excellent way to help yourself through this detox time.

What is 'extreme self-kindness' to you? What kind of things would this include?

How can you add some time to be kind to yourself into your day today?

How can you add some extra kindness time for yourself this week?

Find a way to make today (or a day this weekend) one of those days.

What are some ways you can let yourself relax fully today?

Take a day and let the good stuff you are doing catch up with you. Your body is nineteen days free from alcohol. Reward yourself for this with something that really feels like a treat today.

Self-care is not selfish or self-indulgent.

*We cannot
nurture others from a dry
well.*

*We need to take care of our
own needs first, so
that we can give from our
surplus, our abundance.*

*When we nurture others
from a
place of fullness, we feel
renewed instead of taken
advantage
of.*

-JENNIFER LOUDEN

REFLECTION SPACE

SCRIBBLE, DRAW OR WRITE WHAT'S ON
YOUR MIND TODAY

DAY TWENTY

GOOD THINGS HAPPEN ON THE OTHER SIDE OF HARD.

Day Twenty - Good Things Happen On The Other Side of Hard

This journey of 30 new days can stir up a lot of thoughts about yourself. You could sometimes be struggling with the alcohol-free idea, and then find yourself struggling with the idea that you are having trouble with this. You may be starting to consider what role alcohol has been playing in your life, and if it is a healthy one.

Now that you have completed almost three weeks without alcohol in your system, you can start to look more clearly at the place you want it to be.

For some, the hardest part of this journey is looking back at our past behavior with new eyes. It can be painful to see that when we drank we made decisions, went places and said or did things that we are not so proud of now. It is normal to feel this way, and it is normal for these feelings of regret or sadness to start rising to the surface. Record these thoughts in your journal. But, don't be hard on yourself. Remember this journey is about forward motion, not kicking ourselves about what we did yesterday or last year.

Use the thoughts of your past as the fuel to motivate the change you want. It could be that you now see these past incidents as a reason to limit your drinking in the future or perhaps you want to remove alcohol altogether. Gather the information from your thoughts and allow time to process these things without judgement. Love the journey and what is being uncovered about your actions when you drink.

Spend some time free writing today.
Be gentle and kind to yourself.

Free Writing Space

Doing your best in this moment puts you in the best place for the next moment.

— OPRAH WINFREY

DAY TWENTY-ONE

CREATING NEW PATHWAYS

Day Twenty-One - Creating New Pathways

We all know how easy it is to get in the habit of a glass of wine in the evening, or Friday night drinks out. It is like a well-worn pathway in our brain. We all have certain times when we grab a drink or feel the strong urge to open a bottle of wine and soak in it. Going alcohol-free is about making new pathways and choosing a different way to react to the usual triggers for drinking. It's about finding new solutions to the same problems we would have tried to solve with alcohol.

Part of this journey is to recognize what triggers us the most to want to drink. Have a look at the list of triggers below. Which ones are the strongest for you? Do you have others?

Common triggers:
Overwhelmedness
Anxiety
Boredom
Freedom
Stress
Sadness
Loneliness
Shyness
Excitement
Happiness
Nervousness

Others:

Once we can recognize our trigger, we can start to change our reactions. Instead of being triggered to have a glass of wine, we can use it to trigger a moment of self-care or relaxation. It can take a few attempts to make a new pathway. It takes time to make these new pathways clearer and the more obvious choice when triggered. It is easier to build these new pathways now with a clear mind that is no longer driven by any level of physical withdrawal.

These new pathways can remove the habit of drinking, and the thought that you 'need' a drink. They are about finding a way to let go of the addictive highs and changing the narrative around drinking.

Consider again the list of triggers, in particular the ones that trigger you to want a drink. What is the real need when you feel these emotions? For example, when you feel bored, what do you really want? You want something to do that feels good. What can you do instead of having a drink that will satisfy that desire to do something? Take a bath, go for a run, finish a task or call a friend.

Beside each trigger, write the real need and then an idea of how you can meet that need without a drink.

Overwhelmedness

Anxiety

Boredom

Freedom

Stress

Sadness

Loneliness

Shyness

Excitement

Happiness

Nervousness

Others:

THE BIRD
WHO
DARES TO
FALL
IS THE BIRD
WHO
LEARNS TO
FLY

REFLECTION SPACE

SCRIBBLE, DRAW OR WRITE WHAT'S ON
YOUR MIND TODAY

WEEK THREE REFLECTION

Week Three Reflection

How are you feeling on the scale?

Unhappy	1	2	3	4	5	Happy
Bored	1	2	3	4	5	Excited
Trouble Sleeping	1	2	3	4	5	Sleeping Well
Stressed	1	2	3	4	5	Calm
Unhealthy	1	2	3	4	5	Healthy
Unproductive	1	2	3	4	5	Productive

Describe this week in a few words:

What did you struggle with?

How did you overcome these struggles?

What were the happiest moments of this week?

What did you achieve?

What have you learned about yourself this week?

What would you like to improve next week?

Anything else:

For the next week, I am excited about:

Next week I am looking forward to:

Next week I will be kind to myself and treat myself in the following ways:

Week Four

WEEK FOUR: WHAT TO EXPECT

Week Four: What To Expect

By the end of three alcohol-free weeks, you may be noticing some significant changes. Many people record feeling much more energetic. They notice they are sleeping better and some have even lost a little weight.

Write down what you are feeling or experiencing this week.

What small changes have you noticed?
Look at your face in the mirror. Note any changes you see.

Look at your body. Note any changes you see no matter how small.

Triggers. Have you noticed you can avoid your triggers better?

How?

REFLECTION SPACE

SCRIBBLE, DRAW OR WRITE WHAT'S ON
YOUR MIND TODAY

DAY TWENTY-TWO

CHOOSING NOT TO REACT

Day Twenty-Two - Choosing Not To React

Yesterday we took a closer look at the emotions that can trigger us to drink. What we did not mention is when a trigger is a person or situation. We all have those people and situations that trigger a strong reaction in us. When someone pushes your buttons, an old injustice comes up, or you feel pissed off and annoyed, these can be intense triggers that make us want to enjoy a large glass of wine to take the edge off.

As we discovered yesterday, the key is learning how to change the reaction we have and then choosing a new pathway to take.

Think about a person or situation that really pushes your buttons. Step back from the situation. Look at it from a distance by imagining it happening on a giant movie screen that you are simply watching. As you watch the situation play out in your mind, choose a different way to react. One that the other party would never expect. Withdraw yourself from the situation and imagine someone else in your place reacting in a new way to the trigger. As you sit back and watch this play on the big screen in your mind, add some popcorn and enjoy the show.

Now, when a similar situation arises, the idea of sitting back and watching it with popcorn can be an incredibly helpful way to remove yourself from the usual reaction you would take. Observing, with imaginary popcorn, is an excellent way to deal with people who would usually be a trigger for your drinking. Observe, instead of being triggered to want a drink because of another person's words or behavior.

Describe someone who triggers you in a wrong way:

Do their actions sometimes make you feel like a drink?
Write a little about this.

Is there a way you can avoid this kind of situation?

How can you avoid being triggered by them? Pull out the popcorn!

Is the person someone you need in your life?

It is important to know who to welcome into our lives, and who needs to be shown the door. Focus on the people in your life who make you feel great, build you up, strengthen you and add joy to your life. These are your people!

I choose to remove from my life people who wish to hurt me more than love me, drain me more than replenish me, or pull me down rather than cheer me on.

DAY TWENTY-THREE

DRINKING AWAY INSPIRATION

Day Twenty-Three - Drinking Away Inspiration

Recently, I watched a friend drink away her self-esteem. Throughout the evening, I was astonished to notice that with each glass of wine, she became even more self-critical about her abilities, her work and relationships. She was not a downer. In fact, if you asked her, she was enjoying herself. We were laughing and enjoying our time out. But, I could not help but notice the wine seemed to be sucking away her spark and confidence. Does drinking do this to you?

Have you ever been excited about a project or trying a new thing, then after a few drinks, talked yourself out of trying it? For some, alcohol is actually the opposite of 'Dutch courage'. It can really suck our will to move forward in our life.

Often problems with drinking coincide with issues at work, in our relationships or life in general. We sometimes use these extra stresses as an excuse to drink. But, do we ever stop to think that perhaps the drinking is what was taking away our determination to change our situation? After all, it is easier to relax into a bottle of wine than face the tasks you need to do. We kid ourselves that we will sort those out tomorrow. Did we ever?

Cutting alcohol out of your routine, even for a short time, can free up a whole lot more time, energy and brain space. I certainly spent far too much time and energy worrying about how much I was drinking, wondering if it was too much and if others drank as much. I also noticed that when I drank, my motivation for some of my goals seemed to dip.

Now you have been almost three weeks without drinking, your energy levels may have increased and your positivity also.

What items are on your goal list that you just hadn't had the time and energy to get around to before? Write them down. Now is a great time to bring them out again, dust them off and put some time and energy into them.

Get excited about something new.
Move the focus off drinking for a while and put some of this new energy into a new project.

Define
success on your own terms,
achieve it by your own rules,
and build a life you are proud to live

- ANNE SWEENEY

DAY TWENTY-FOUR

THE MOMENTUM OF NOT DRINKING

Day Twenty-Four - The Momentum Of Not Drinking

By this point of your 30-day alcohol-free journey, you may be getting quite used to not drinking. The physical cravings should have passed, and it is only the thoughts of drinking that make you want one. There is no longer any substance your body is longing for.

You are into the last week of this 30-day alcohol-free journey. And, you might be starting to look forward to breaking your alcohol-free fast. It could also be that you are enjoying the momentum of not drinking, and have decided it fits your lifestyle better.

Now is a great time to have a look at how you feel after three weeks without drinking.

Do you feel better when you don't drink?

Would you consider trying this alcohol-free journey for longer? 60 days, or perhaps even 100 days? Write down your thoughts about this:

It could be that you are still in two minds about this. Could it be that not drinking is something you would like to try for a longer term? In that case, now is the time to listen to that voice and build on the momentum you have now.

You have a clear mind. Your body is back in the natural balance it was born to be in. Your cravings are no longer physical, and your mood may have balanced out. These are all great things and a great place to be in.

TAKE CONTROL OF YOUR CHOICE TO DRINK OR NOT.
Write down your decision here:

FORWARD
MOMENTUM.

THAT'S MY
NEW MOTTO.

NO REGRETS.
AND NO GOING
BACK.

— GAYLE FORMAN

DAY TWENTY-FIVE

A GOOD EXCUSE IS STILL JUST AN EXCUSE

Day Twenty-Five - A Good Excuse Is Still Just An Excuse

Over the last three weeks, you have taken control of the choices you make around drinking. You have chosen not to drink and made it your responsibility to follow through on your promise to yourself.

You would have encountered times when it would have been easy to drink and when it would have been easy to give in to the circumstances and stop this journey.

There is a whole world of pressure and marketing around alcohol that tells us we need this drink. It is in the messages that 'Mummy needs wine', or 'you earned that beer'.

We have been taught that drinking is the thing we do when we are celebrating, relaxing, getting over heartbreak, finished with a tough day at work, because it is wine o'clock, to de-stress, to get our buzz on, to be social, to be alone, etc.

Now, by learning to make choices and not let the external situations dictate your actions, you have stopped playing victim to alcohol. You can see through the hype and know that a good excuse is still just an excuse to drink. If you don't want to drink, there should be no excuse good enough to tempt you to drink. If, however, you are looking for a reason to drink, you will easily find one because billions of dollars of advertising budgets have ensured they have every reason covered and a drink for every occasion.

Stop giving in to excuses! Stop being a victim of your excuses, and keep control over whether you drink or not. The choice is fully yours.

When it starts to become challenging to keep going, that is when the real work begins, and you can learn the most about yourself. Be willing to try things you would not normally do. Experience something different, choose a different reaction, and try a new way of coping. If you want to ensure alcohol is not playing too big a part in your life, then dare to remove it from the situations when you have always used it. If it is not essential, remove it.

What excuses to drink have you most commonly used in the past?

Are these just excuses?

Use this space to write about the reasons you would have wanted a drink in the past:

Use this space to write about how you feel about those reasons now:

When you
repeat a mistake,
it is not a
mistake anymore;
it is a decision

- PAULO COELHO

DAY TWENTY-SIX

THE IMPORTANCE OF CONNECTION

Day Twenty-Six - The Importance Of Connection

A sober curious journey can be a little lonely. You may have felt disconnected from the people you would usually spend time with. Most likely because you always saw them when drinking. Your habits and the way you spend your time have changed over these past few weeks.

A connection with others is so important in our lives. It is a great time now to reach out to people you have lost contact with.
Get connected. Find some communities to interact with.

What things do you do that are guaranteed to make you feel great?
E.g. going for a walk, catching up with friends, or drawing.
Write down 3 -5 things.

What things do you like to do that give you a sense of achievement?
E.g. cleaning the kitchen, gardening, or finishing a task.
Write down 3-5 things.

Find ways to add these things to your week and invite a friend to join you. Or, just invite a friend to go for a walk or catch up without alcohol. Consider sharing your achievement of 26 days without drinking with them.

"I don't need a friend who
changes when I change
and who nods when I
nod; my shadow does
that much
better."

– PLUTARCH

DAY TWENTY-SEVEN

KNOCKED OFF BALANCE

Day Twenty-Seven - Knocked Off Balance

What is the strongest emotion that makes you want to have a drink? For me, it is frustration. I am a person with a tremendous amount of energy and forward motion. When I set a goal, I want to dive in and get on with it. When my progression towards that goal is halted or held up for some reason, my internal frustration grows. I feel blocked. Unable to move forward. I feel anger at the thing stopping me. And, I feel like a drink.

Why? Because I am uncomfortable experiencing that feeling of frustration and I want to numb it. When I do not drink, I have to experience that feeling.

I have to realize that sometimes it is our turn to sit and wait. We cannot always respond and move forward when and how we want. It is not a big problem. Pushing makes me feel grumpy, unwell, unbalanced, and so does drinking. I am learning to relax, wait to respond and stop stripping the gears to get forward. Drinking makes it more challenging to maintain a balance.

Removing the drink allows us to move away from extreme emotions and enables us to walk the middle path.

What knocks you off balance? Write down the things that get under your skin, or set you on a downward spin.

What emotions do these things bring up?

What emotion makes you want to drink?

What is it about this emotion? Why does it make you feel like this?

Is there a way you can be comfortable sitting in this emotion? How?

Look at the list of things that irritate you. Are there things on that list that need to change or go?

Only when we are brave enough to explore the darkness will we discover the infinite power of
OUR LIGHT

- BRENE BROWN

REFLECTION SPACE

SCRIBBLE, DRAW OR WRITE WHAT'S ON
YOUR MIND TODAY

DAY TWENTY-EIGHT

I DESERVE A DRINK

Day Twenty-Eight - I Deserve a Drink

Why do we drink? I can only answer this for me. I know that much of my desire to drink is about taking a break from a busy life. It is about feeling relaxed. It is also about being independently me, not wanting to answer to anyone else for a while.

The marketing geniuses of the world have led us to believe that a glass of wine is an escape; it is something we have earned from our busy lives of being everything to everyone. They have sold us a glass of wine as a way to have a small portion of time and space for ourselves. Yet, as we have learned over the last 27 days, a glass of wine can also take so much away from us. Drinking can suck in your health, confidence and ambition.

Why then do we believe that a glass of wine is something we are entitled to have at the end of a busy day when the kids are finally asleep or when we make dinner or when we enjoy a night out? Wouldn't these be better times to indulge in ultimate self-care with things that nourish and build us up? Instead, we are encouraged by society to use alcohol to relax. A drug that quickly gets under our skin, out of control and robs us of what we work so hard to get.

Over these past 27 days, you have been unpacking many of the stories and habits you have around drinking. Before, did you also view a drink as something we earn after a busy day?

Has your view of 'I deserve a drink' changed over the last 28 days? How?

If we want alcohol to become a smaller part of our lives, or have no place in our lives, we need to let go of the old ideas we have around it. We need to create new ones.

Instead of 'I deserve a drink', write down some things you deserve at the end of a busy day. E.g. I deserve to put my feet up and watch Netflix.

You have a
new story to write
and it looks
nothing like your
past

WEEK FOUR REFLECTION

Week Four Reflection

Unhappy   1   2   3   4   5   Happy

Bored   1   2   3   4   5   Excited

Trouble Sleeping   1   2   3   4   5   Sleeping Well

Stressed   1   2   3   4   5   Calm

Unhealthy   1   2   3   4   5   Healthy

Unproductive   1   2   3   4   5   Productive

Describe this week in a few words:

What did you struggle with?

How did you overcome these struggles?

What were the happiest moments of this week?

What did you achieve?

What have you learned about yourself this week?

What would you like to improve next week?

Anything else:

For the next week, I am excited about:

Next week I am looking forward to:

Next week I will be kind to myself and treat myself in the following ways:

DAY TWENTY-NINE

HOW AWESOME THIS IS

Day Twenty-Nine - How Awesome This is

Have you taken time to think about how great it is to have made it to 29 days of being alcohol-free? Even if you have missed a day, you made it through something that many people struggle with. If your drinking has been worrying you, this achievement is proof that you can and are willing to do something about it.

Did you encounter an event or occasion in the last 29 days when you would typically have drunk alcohol? Describe the event:

How do you feel about getting through this without drinking?
I hope you feel proud of yourself.

After a weekend away with friends who were also old drinking buddies, I felt amazing to have enjoyed a fantastic weekend away without drinking once. It was challenging and confronting at times, and, of course, I wanted to drink like old times. But sitting in the airport on my way home, I remember feeling great, energetic, happy and so very glad that I didn't drink all weekend.

I love the learning and growth that happens over 30 days without drinking. I love the journey of exploring our beliefs and finding the ones that no longer fit our lives. Challenging our assumptions around drinking is a fantastic way to grow, evolve and learn about ourselves.

In what ways have you felt challenged by this time?

What positive shifts have occurred in your thinking about drinking?

What challenges you now about drinking?

Find all the
beliefs that stop
you from
achieving your
dreams and let
them go.

DAY THIRTY

YOU WRITE YOUR ROAD

Day Thirty - You Write Your Road

You have reached the goal of 30 days without drinking. Your perspective on your drinking habits is now forever changed. Where you go from here is up to you.

You get to write the road ahead now. Will you continue this alcohol-free journey and make it a three-month, one-year or lifelong journey? Are you ready to walk on further and see what lies ahead on this cleaner, non-toxic life? The choice is yours.

Whatever you choose after this 30-day journey, plan to give yourself all the love, self-care and time you need. Do your best to remember to stop when you need to, relax when you need to and remove yourself from situations you need to.

I WRITE THE ROAD

As I move on from 30 days alcohol-free…

I want to be:

I want to do:

I want to go:

I want to see:

I want to try:

TWO ROADS
DIVERGED IN THE
WOODS AND I,
I TOOK THE ONE
LEAST TRAVELED BY,
AND,
THAT HAS
MADE ALL THE
DIFFERENCE.

30 NEW DAYS REFLECTION

30 New Days Reflection

Unhappy	1 2 3 4 5	Happy
Bored	1 2 3 4 5	Excited
Trouble Sleeping	1 2 3 4 5	Sleeping Well
Stressed	1 2 3 4 5	Calm
Unhealthy	1 2 3 4 5	Healthy
Unproductive	1 2 3 4 5	Productive

This is your final day for reflection. It is time to look back at all the past reflections you have completed.

Looking back at the first few days of this journal is an important part of finishing this journey with clarity. It is now likely to be 30 days since you last experienced a hangover or the effects of alcohol. Your body is probably feeling pretty great, and your mind is a lot clearer. The time that has passed has been great for getting a new habit formed.

The downside of the time that has passed is that our memories of the not-so-great parts of drinking have started to fade. We forget why we started this journey in the first place. By looking back over the past journal entries, you can begin to get a feeling for the difference between now and then. This is important as you look ahead to the next steps after your 30 New Days alcohol-free journey.

Look back over the past reflection pages.

Has your happiness score changed since the first week?

Has your level of excitement changed?

How have your sleeping patterns changed?

Has your stress level changed?

Has your feeling of health changed?

Has your level of productivity changed?

Describe this journey in three words:

What did you struggle with?

What did you learn?

What would you like to improve?

What was your biggest achievement in this 30 New Days?

What was your biggest hurdle?

How did you overcome it?

Think ahead to the coming days after this journey and how you feel about the future.

I am excited to:

I am looking forward to:

DAY 30+

Day 30+

Today is the day! You have reached the goal of 30 days alcohol-free. If you have missed a day or slipped up during this journey, still be happy that you have been sober curious for 30 days.

During this journey, you have uncovered beliefs and stories in your life that no longer fit you. You have changed, moved onwards, expanded new possibilities and had a sober curious adventure.

Now it is up to you to decide what is next. It is the perfect time to use the momentum of this achievement to spur you forward into the next adventure of change - whatever that is for you. By reaching a goal, we tell ourselves that we are a priority and that we want the best for ourselves.

This 30-day journey has been about relentless forward motion, moving onwards and upwards. I hope it has encouraged you to explore expanding other possibilities in life and do it with joy, kindness and no regrets.

WHAT NEXT?

This 30-day detox from alcohol has created some space between you and drinking. In this time and space, you have been able to explore your relationship with alcohol and see it with more clarity.

This journey could be all that was needed to 'reset' the place alcohol had in your life. These 30 days may have been just enough time for you to find the balance that you were looking for.

You may have found this time was the perfect way to feel better and healthier after a period of overindulging.

It can also be the case that these 30 days have highlighted some real issues you have with drinking. It may have brought up things about your use of alcohol that you are no longer comfortable with. This 30-day journey could be the start of entirely rethinking the place alcohol has in your life. It could be the beginning of a longer journey towards more balance, awareness, and a time to change.

From this point, you will be deciding what to do next. Will you start drinking again or not?

You may be weighing up the pros and cons of moderation, so I wanted to offer a few thoughts to help you with the decision.

To Moderate or Abstain

When trying to decide if you will move forward from here by continuing to abstain from drinking or by moderating your intake, consider these ideas:

Separate emotion and old habits from the decision

Don't let stress, anxiety or pressure from friends, family or loved ones influence your decision. Remember the triggers that made you want to drink before and keep them out of this decision.
Feelings like anger, frustration, sadness or loneliness can trigger a desire to be drunk again.

Ask yourself if this time will be different

You started this journey because there was something about your drinking habits that bothered you. How will this time be different?

Plan

If you have decided to follow a path of moderation, plan it well.

What will moderation look like for you?

How many drinks per day/week/month?

How much energy and brain time is moderation going to cost you?

I.e. will you require yourself to ask the following each time you drink:

What should I drink?

How much is too much?

Should I have another one?

Have I had too many this week?

Consider the effort

Be aware that moderation can be tough to follow. If you have had a bad day or just feel a little stressed, it can be too much to deal with. We all know the nature of alcohol and that we only crave more. Reintroducing alcohol, even in moderation, can easily restart a cycle of wanting more.

Think back to how much you were drinking before you started this journey.

Would you say it was too much? Just right?

.

Will you go back to that level again? How quickly?

Is that level of drinking OK for you?

There is a famous saying among the sober movement:

> One drink is too much, and one thousand drinks are not enough.

AVOID THE SLIPPERY SLOPE

For many, the first drink is a slippery slope that can land them back to where they started. If you embarked on this journey because your level of drinking was uncomfortable for you, you might want to think again about that first drink.

After a few drinks, we all know that our willpower can fly right out the window. Making a rule only to have two glasses of wine is harder to keep when the second glass is finished, and there is still half a bottle of wine in the fridge. We all know this feeling.

Are you going to hate yourself if moderation fails? I recall failing many times at moderation and waking up in the middle of the night hating my lack of willpower, my inability to restrict myself to only one glass of wine. It is like the nectar of the wine just draws me in, and I want to soak in it glass after glass. But, inevitably, I am annoyed at myself for this the next morning.

IT DOESN'T HAVE TO BE BLACK AND WHITE

If you feel that moderation is the best thing for you, take a step into it. Give it a good try and see if it works. If it doesn't, there is no shame in making another attempt at detox.

If you are not ready to make a decision yet, put it off for another 30 days. Keep the momentum of not drinking going by remaining alcohol-free for another 30 days. When you get to the 60-day mark, see how you feel about this decision. Maybe 100 days is a good goal for now.

CHOOSING TO ABSTAIN

Many people find moderation simply too exhausting. They decide that the easier path for them is not to drink. By making a single choice not to drink, they avoid having to make a million more decisions about their drinking. If you are sure that alcohol has no place in your life, then you can make the decision now not to drink again. I have included in the back of this book a list of great resources, courses and books that can help you further on this journey.

Whatever your decision is from this point, I want to thank you for taking this leg of the journey with me through this book. I wish you much joy, happiness and endless wonder at the changes 30 days can make.

LIFE DOES NOT
GET BETTER
BY CHANCE, IT
GETS BETTER BY
CHANGE.
–ROHN

DETOX HELP SECTION

Detox Help Section

The Detox Help Section is filled with practical ideas and advice for getting through 30 days alcohol-free. Refer back to this section when you need some new ideas, practical support or further information about your detox journey.

DETOX TIMELINE

Detox Timeline

The most common questions about starting this 30-day alcohol-free journey are about the detox timeline. It takes around seven-ten days for alcohol to be physically out of your system. Here is a summary of what you can expect during detox.

Day One

As soon as the alcohol hits your bloodstream, your body begins the process of removing it. During the first few hours after drinking, your liver begins working to clear the alcohol from your blood and prevent alcohol poisoning. At the same time, your pancreas starts producing extra insulin to help the process. This is why we often crave heavy carbs like pizza when we drink.

At around 12 hours after drinking your last drink, your blood sugar should be back to normal levels. But, your body will be dehydrated due to the diuretic effect of alcohol. Drinking a lot more water will help reduce dehydration and assist in clearing the alcohol from your system.

As you will know, within a few hours of stopping drinking, you will experience headaches, tiredness, grumpiness – all the usual hangover stuff.

DAY TWO

The main hangover symptoms will have peaked now. If you have been drinking heavily, you may start to feel some other uncomfortable symptoms such as a rapid heartbeat, change in blood pressure, or sweating. It is very important to note here that if these symptoms become severe or if you begin to experience tremors, confusion and hallucinations, convulsions, blackouts or fever, please contact your health professional immediately for further medical assistance to get through this detox. These symptoms may be what is called delirium tremens or DTs. While uncommon, this is a severe condition that requires medical intervention. Heavy drinkers who suddenly stop drinking can experience a range of dangerous symptoms and need a medically-assisted detox.

For most of us, the alcohol will be out of our bloodstream by the end of the day. This is when withdrawal symptoms can appear.

COMMON WITHDRAWAL SYMPTOMS

Nervousness

Fatigue

Anxiety

Irritability

Insomnia

Clammy skin

Vomiting

To help with feeling unwell during this time, try sipping ginger or peppermint tea. Both are fantastic for settling your stomach and reducing nausea.

DAY THREE – SIX

From day three, the withdrawal symptoms will reduce. You may be starting to feel normal again. This is not to say you will not experience cravings, but simply that some of the acute physical withdrawal symptoms will have disappeared.
You may still experience occasional headaches, anxiety, and/or irritability. Some people even experience weird nightmares or dream that they have accidentally had a drink.

It is normal at this time to feel sad, angry, or resentful. After all, you're giving up something you believe you enjoy. Working through this 30 New Days journal will help you process these feelings and find the joy in this journey.

After one week without drinking, you are likely to be sleeping better. When we drink, we often miss the full refreshing sleep that our bodies need. Once your sleeping patterns improve, you will notice you have more energy and focus. If you are experiencing insomnia, I have included more information on how to cope with this in the section on Difficulty Sleeping.

After a week of not drinking, your skin will already be looking better. Alcohol causes severe dehydration, and our skin is the first place where this is noticeable. Skin conditions such as dandruff, eczema, and rosacea will begin to improve with the extra hydration.

After two weeks without the extra calories of alcohol, many start to notice they are losing weight, and their digestion improved. Other significant effects of two weeks without alcohol are higher energy levels, less fatigue and clearer skin. Most negative symptoms of withdrawal will have finished. Headaches, nausea and hungover feelings will have eased now.

From week three onwards, you are likely to notice positive improvements in your overall mood. There is a marked decrease in overall anxiety and depression. This is combined with much higher levels of mental clarity, improved memory, better concentration, increased sense of connection, decreased levels of stress, higher self-esteem, greater motivation and a more positive outlook on life in general. It is all good news.

From week three, the whole detox can seem much more manageable. The extra energy and positive vibes make it easier to make healthier choices, choose better foods, drink more water, do more exercise, and get more sleep.

AFTER 30 DAYS

After one month without alcohol in your system, the fat in your liver reduces by around 15% on average, increasing its ability to filter toxins out of the body. Many notice a reduction in weight and especially belly fat. Overall, you are likely to be sleeping better and finding it easier to fall asleep and stay asleep.

AFTER ONE YEAR OF BEING ALCOHOL-FREE

After one year of being alcohol-free, most people lose a significant amount of belly fat. The risk of cancers of the mouth, liver and breast reduces.

The secret of
change is to
focus all of your
energy, not on
the old,
but on building
the new.

DIFFICULTY SLEEPING

Difficulty Sleeping

During your 30 New Days Alcohol-Free Journey, you may have nights when it is difficult to fall asleep. Insomnia is a normal part of the detoxifying process, and can really get you down. However, there are some simple things you can do to minimize this problem.

First, it is essential to understand that alcohol was not been helping you sleep well. Alcohol is a known depressant that numbs our brains. While a few glasses of wine can relax you and help you get to sleep quicker, having alcohol in our bloodstream hinders our natural sleep pattern. When you have had a drink or two, your sleep is disrupted and does not go through the normal six sleep cycles we need at night.

Secondly, when we drink before bed, our bodies get busy processing that alcohol and this action prevents us from falling into a deep, restful sleep. When you drink regularly, you are continuously missing out on the deep refreshing sleep your body needs. This leads to feeling drained and distracted the next day.

Drinking regularly leaves us operating in a sleep-deprived condition. This is also why most people will notice a dramatic increase in energy after the first couple of weeks of not drinking.

Until your normal sleep habits kick in again, you may need some help getting to sleep. Here are my top tips for easing the pain of sleeplessness:

REDUCE CAFFEINE

If you are like me and need a good cup of coffee to wake up, try to limit it to two or three cups spaced over the morning and early afternoon. Ditch the coffee and caffeinated drinks after 2 p.m. Try switching a coffee for tea or hot chocolate instead.

RELAXATION STRETCHES

Try some relaxation exercises before bed. A simple yoga stretch or a breathing exercise can help your body to relax and get ready for bed.

INCREASE YOUR EXERCISE

Up your level of exercise during the day. Getting some exercise during the day can work wonders for making us feel sleepy in the evening. Go for a walk before you start your day or take an after-dinner walk around your neighborhood. An evening stroll is a fantastic way to wind down naturally.

READ BEFORE BED

Read an actual book. Switch off the devices in your bedroom and get comfy instead with a good book. Escape into another world and let your mind switch off from your day.

HAVE A HOT BUBBLE BATH

Pamper yourself with a deep, hot bubble bath. Light some candles, and relax in the bath with a book and a cup of tea.

ZONE OUT

Put on some quiet music, an audiobook, a podcast or some white noise as you lie in bed. Quietly listening will signal your body that it can relax and doze off to sleep.

TAKE NOTES

Have a notebook by your bed. When you wake up in the night with something on your mind, write it down so you can act on it in the morning. This will allow your mind to let the thought go and get back to sleep.

DON'T LIE AWAKE

If you wake up in the night and simply cannot get back to sleep, don't lie there worrying about it. Turn on your light and read a book for a few minutes until you feel sleepy again. Or, get up and make yourself a warm milk drink and relax on your sofa for half an hour or so until you feel sleepy and ready to go back to bed.

COOL DOWN

Allow your body to cool down. Throw off your blankets for a few minutes and let your body temperature drop a little. This can help induce a sleepy feeling.

MAKE IT DARK

Make sure your room is dark and cool. Cover any digital clocks or other electronic devices that emit light.

JUST REST

If you are lying awake, remind yourself that even resting is good. Avoid getting into an anxiety spiral of not being able to fall asleep.

PICK

WHAT

MAKES

YOU

HAPPY

DETOX SURVIVAL KIT

Detox Survival Kit

Your personal detox survival kit is made up of all the things that make you feel happy and relaxed. It is a collection of items and ideas that help you manage cravings and withdrawal symptoms calmly and effectively.

This list is made up of things that helped me and others through this time. Pick and choose what will work for you, and/or add your own items. You are making your personal survival kit. So, make it perfect for you!

PHYSICAL ITEMS:

Vitamin, mineral and herbal supplements
Useful dietary supplements include B-group vitamins, vitamin C, zinc and magnesium.

Essential oils
Your favorite essential oils in a roll-on or burner to use when you have cravings.

Homeopathic remedies

Physical reminders
A charm bracelet or chain that reminds you to stay strong

Herbal teas
Some favorites to try are lemon tea, green tea, Yogi bedtime tea, ginger and orange tea.

Books
I have included a list of great books at the back of this book.

Snacks

Keep a handy supply of your choice of healthy or sweet snacks to eat when a craving hits.

Water

A large bottle of sparkling or still water.

Awesome playlist

TECHNIQUES/ACTIVITIES: ALL THE THINGS YOU COULD DO INSTEAD OF DRINKING

Yoga

YouTube or classes

Breathing techniques

Spiritual practices

Meditation or praying

Exercise

Walking, running, yoga, pilates, cycling, swimming

Cooking yummy food

Buying yummy food

Sleeping as much as you want

Binge-watching

Netflix, HBO, or your favorite TV channel

Bubble baths

Decluttering
Cleaning, spring cleaning, throwing stuff out

Gardening

Reading
There is a list of great books in the helpful resources section.

Getting outside

ATTITUDES:

Give yourself a break
Perfection isn't required for this journey. If the bed isn't made or the kitchen bench is a mess, let it go for now.

Ask for support
Let some people know you are making this 30-day journey and let them give you some support too.

OOPS
I HAD A
DRINK

Oops I Had A Drink

Please do not panic if you have had a drink today. There is no need to beat yourself up about not completing this 30-day journey correctly. This journey is not about perfection; it is about forward momentum and exploring the idea of being alcohol-free.

Don't punish yourself by beginning again at day one. Keep moving forward to the next day as usual. If you had a drink last night, just get up this morning and move on. Remember the 30 New Days goal is to create forward momentum towards your goal. This takes place over the whole 30 days, and any misstep is simply part of this journey to discover more about your relationship with alcohol. Starting at the beginning again is disheartening, punishing and unnecessary.

On this journey, there are no mistakes, only breakthroughs.
If you have had a drink, and now feel guilty or bad about it, please don't. Instead, take the time to think about what made you want to drink.

Were you sad? Lonely? Excited? Describe your mood before drinking here:

What triggered you to reach for a drink? Take note of it here:

Who

Where

What

Why

How

Read what you have written above again. These are your trigger points. They are the clues to what makes you want to drink. Try to explore these a little deeper.

Why did you feel triggered by these things?

Turn this small difficulty into a lesson that will help you next time you encounter a similar situation. Remember you are trying something new out. It is like a training period. Don't beat yourself up if you have a drink. Success is always built on failure. We do not strive for perfection over these 30 new days. Instead, the focus is on the journey, the curiosity of what it means not to drink. Then, get back to the business of your 30 days.

Know that you are not alone in slipping up, most people do. The point of difference is whether you give up now or if you get back to your goal of finishing these 30 new days alcohol-free.

The following phrases are useful to remind yourself of this journey's purpose:

I don't have any regrets.

This was an experience I don't want to repeat.

I will learn from this and move forward.

I am so grateful for this lesson.

I would rather feel the sting of this lesson and learn, than give up and forever feel the pain of regret.

I will focus on the lessons not the mistakes.

ON THIS
JOURNEY, THERE
ARE NO
MISTAKES,
ONLY
BREAKTHROUGHS

HELPFUL RESOURCES

Helpful Resources

COURSES:

Tempest Sobriety School
https://www.jointempest.com/

Tempest Sobriety School is an 8-week virtual course. Offering daily thoughts or meditations to help you set your intention for the day as well as weekly lectures to uncover how alcohol shows up in various aspects of your life. The course includes Q+A calls and small breakout groups to help you digest and process the course materials.

The Alcohol Experiment https://thisnakedmind.com/programs-training/

The Alcohol Experiment, run by Annie Grace, author of *The Naked Mind*, offers a judgment-free action plan for anyone who's ever wondered what life without alcohol is like. The rules are simple: Abstain from drinking for 30 days and just see how you feel. Annie arms her readers with the science-backed information to address the cultural and emotional conditioning we experience around alcohol. The result is a mindful approach that puts you back in control and permanently stops cravings.

Hip Sobriety

https://www.hipsobriety.com/

Hip Sobriety explores Holly Whitaker's journey to sobriety and the writing of her bestselling book, *Quit Like A Woman.*

Unpickled Blog

https://unpickledblog.com/

"How I secretly quit my secret habit of secretly drinking." – Jean

Living Sober

https://livingsober.org.nz/

The friendliest community to talk safely and honestly with others about your relationship with alcohol.

Soberistas – Love life in control

https://soberistas.com/

The Soberistas community is all about giving up alcohol and living a life in control.

Sober Nation – Putting Recovery on the map

https://sobernation.com/

Join the recovery revolution for networking, support, resources and community.

PODCASTS:

The Bubble Hour

https://www.blogtalkradio.com/bubblehour

The Bubble Hour is hosted by Jean M., a sober woman dedicated to breaking down the walls of stigma and denial surrounding alcoholism.

Since Right Now – Addiction Recovery Podcast

http://sincerightnow.com/

An entertaining, thoughtful, insightful and authentic podcast. "The podcast your sponsor warned you about."

Recovery Elevator – Find Your Better You

https://www.recoveryelevator.com/podcasts/

The Recovery Elevator podcast has a clear goal: to shred the shame. Alcoholism is a disease and alcohol is one of the most addictive and dangerous drugs on the planet. It's time to start talking about this.

The Unruffled Podcast – Art and Recovery

https://soundcloud.com/stevehecht-561628099

The Unruffled Podcast explores all topics relating to creativity in recovery. Learn how to thrive.

This Naked Mind: Control Alcohol – Annie Grace

This Naked Mind is about finding freedom from alcohol. It helps you remove psychological dependence and ensure that *you will not crave alcohol*, allowing you to easily drink less (or stop drinking).

Quit Like a Woman - Holly Whitaker

This honest and witty book, *Quit Like a Woman,* is a groundbreaking look at our drinking culture. It offers a roadmap to cutting out alcohol in order to live our best lives without it. You may never look at drinking the same way again after reading this book.

The Unexpected Joy of Being Sober: **Discovering a happy, healthy, wealthy alcohol-free life** – Catherine Gray

In *The Unexpected Joy of Being Sober*, Catherine Gray examines society's drink-pushing and discovers more about why we drink. This book is about the escape, and why a sober life can be more intoxicating than you ever imagined.

Quit Drinking Without Willpower: **Be a happy Non-drinker**
– Allen Carr

In *Quit Drinking Without Willpower*, Allen Carr explains why you feel the need to drink, and then with simple step-by-step instructions works to set you free. An excellent book for anyone wanting escape from the alcohol trap for good.

We Are the Luckiest: **The Surprising Magic of a Sober Life**
– Laura McKowen

This straight-talking book is filled with personal stories, addressing issues such as facing facts, the question of AA, and other people's drinking. Without sugarcoating the difficulty of becoming sober, she highlights the many blessings of sobriety.

MORE GREAT BOOKS TO EXPLORE BEYOND SOBRIETY:

The Great Work of Your Life: A Guide for the Journey to Your True Calling – Stephen Cope

The Great Work of Your Life is an inspiring guide to uncovering your life's purpose.

The Dark Side of the Light Chasers: Reclaiming Your Power, Creativity, Brilliance and Dreams – Debbie Ford

Debbie Ford leads the reader through stories and exercises in *The Dark Side of the Light Chasers* to help us recognize our hidden emotions, and how to find the gifts they offer us.

***The Four Agreements*: A Practical Guide to Personal Freedom (A Toltec Wisdom Book)** – Paul Miguel Ruiz

In *The Four Agreements*, Don Miguel Ruiz explains how our self-limiting beliefs can rob us of joy and create suffering. He instead offers a powerful code of conduct that can transform lives and offer a new experience of freedom, true happiness, and love.

NEXT STEPS...

Next Steps…

If you enjoyed this journey and are looking for more articles and information about change, you can find more on the 30 New Days website: www.30NewDays.com.

Find out more at www.30newdays.com
Follow and join the conversations:
Instagram: @30newdays
Facebook: 30NewDays

MORE 30 NEW DAYS BOOKS

More 30 New Days Books

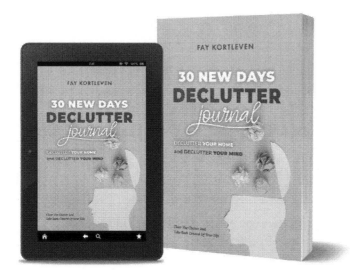

30 New Days Declutter Journal: Declutter Your Home and Declutter Your Mind – Fay Kortleven

This is the clutter intervention you have been looking for. Find out how clutter holds you back and keeps you stuck, then do something about it. This life-changing decluttering workbook makes real life organizing easy.

Declutter your mind as you declutter your space. Get organized, get focused and get clarity.

The 30 New Days Declutter Journal is your daily prompt to help you organize your space, your life and your mind in 30 easy days.

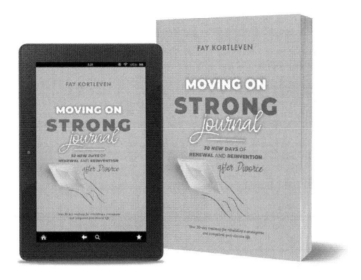

Moving On Strong Journal: 30 New Days of Renewal and Reinvention After Divorce – Fay Kortleven

The Moving On Strong Journal presents 30 daily readings and writing prompts for relentless forward motion towards identifying and achieving your goals. This journal is designed to help you through this life-changing event with kindness and encouragement.

Moving on Strong is a guided journal that has been created with kindness and love to inspire you each day without bullying, pushing or tough love. Inside you will find tonnes of love and encouragement to help you find your feet again after the pain of a separation. There are lots of spaces to write, reflect and record your journey.